Kie

Ingredients

For

Success

The Boss Lady Handbook

Kierra Alderman

Copyright © 2019 Kierra Alderman.

All rights reserved. No part of this book may be used or reproduced by any means, graphic, electronic, or mechanical, including photocopying, recording, taping or by any information storage retrieval system without written permission of the author, except in the case of brief quotations embodied in critical articles and reviews.

ISBN: 978-1-7330657-4-0

WEB: usempowerment.com, bolempowerment.com

Contents

Contents	3
WELCOME OBJECTIVE	6
Mission	13
Kie Ingredient 1	15
Take charge of your kitchen!	15
Kie Ingredient 2	28
Mindset	28
Kie Ingredient 3	43
Pay attention to detail	43
Kie Ingredient 4	57
Measure	57
Kie Ingredient 5	75
Be prepared to make a disastrous meal!	
	75
Kle Ingredient 6	89

Preparation 89

PLANNING AND ORGANIZATION OF TIME 90

Kie Ingredient 7 100

Cooking 100

Kie Ingredient 8 104

THE PERCEPTION IN THE WORK AREA 105

Kie Ingredient 9 113

Keep a close eye on what your cooking 113

Adjust The Fire and Stir To Keep From Burning: Characteristics of a Toxic Work Environment 116

You Can't Open The Oven For Certain Foods: Consequences 124

Kie Ingredient 10 131

Gathering your seasonings	131
Kie Ingredient 11	145
Setting the table	145
Kie Ingredient 12	154
Pay attention to the recipe	154

Welcome Objective

Congratulations!!!! I am ecstatic you have chosen to step into the kitchen with KIS (Kie Ingredients for Success). This book will force you to step into your "Enhancement Kitchen" and select your own Kie Ingredients. These ingredients will help you formulate YOUR own recipe for success! I cannot tell you how many times I hear, "What's your secret to success?" For years I kept telling people that there was no secret, until one day, after years of speaking with successful individuals, it finally hit me that there was. There was indeed a secret to being successful, and I am not talking about being rich or anything monetary in nature, but actual success. Whether it was at work, relationships, schools, or just everyday life, people and especially women, all carried a deep-rooted secret to their success.

I come from a very large family, my grandmother Sylvia had fifteen children, so I am being modest when I tell you that my family and I started from humble beginnings. Having fifteen children meant that my grandmother was not able to afford certain luxuries, such as dining out, but it also meant that she became an all-star in the kitchen. I spent many years in the kitchen with my grandmother, being a thorn in her side while trying to master her recipes, however, despite the fact that I followed her ingredients to a T, my dishes never tasted quite the same. I found myself continuously asking her, "what's your secret, there has to be a secret ingredient that you aren't telling me about"; to which she would politely chuckle and always respond with the same way "a pinch of love."

This book will be used to not only help you discover which Kie Ingredients you already possess, but it will also help you determine which ingredient you should invest in. My aim is to help you be successful in the job market specifically, but please know that many of these ingredients and principles can be applied to various aspects of your everyday life. Although I will be providing you with a basic recipe for success, the finished product will be completely your own because YOU are the secret ingredient! Just like every other famous recipe, or those that register more closely to home like my grandmother's recipes, there is always a secret ingredient. Simply adding a pinch of this, or a dab of that, can completely change the flavor. YOU are that pinch or dab!

My journey towards success has been completely paved with obstacles, but it is a journey that I wouldn't trade for the world, because it provided me with an abundance of ingredients, and allowed me to make some phenomenal recipes. Everyone's journey and experiences are completely their own, which is the strongest tool in your arsenal because it means that no one else will be able to duplicate your recipe, because you are unique. It is important to understand that being authentically you will help you to compose the most flavorsome dish.

I am elated to have the opportunity to empower and motivate women from all walks of life, especially those who have a longing for leadership. It's no secret that in society, and some organizations, women are still considered the "weaker sex." This can be reflected through salaries or requirements/restraints placed on a position. Some organizations believe that maternity, or family life, can limit women and hinder their commitment and decision making in the company. However, this is far from the truth! Today more women than previously are moving into the labor market, and standing shoulder to shoulder with their male peers. Women are finding themselves with the ambition and objective to drive corporations to provide better products and services for customers and consumers.

The advantages of adding women to business management are proven. In a study by the consultant McKinsey, it was shown that companies with women in management positions generate a higher gross profit of 47.6%, compared to those that have men in the high ranks. The research was carried out in 303 large companies in Latin America.

Women stand out for their intrinsic characteristics such as intuition, empathy, versatility, and communication in work environments. These attributes they demonstrate in their interpersonal relationships are also linked to their responsibilities and work commitments. Those companies that consider women for managerial positions will undoubtedly have a better work environment and greater long-term productivity.

Mission

> *My mission in life is to remain authentic to myself, my heritage, and my founding principles. I must remind myself that although sugar and salt bear similar resemblance, the taste each ingredient carries are completely contradictory from one another. Which is why conformity will never suit me. If I am salt, I will never pass myself off as sugar, and if I am sugar, I will never pass myself off as salt because no one wants a sugary steak, or a salty cake.*

In short, I am more than what meets the eye. You can't see my flavor!

My goal is to offer you ingredients that:

- Aid you in identifying long term & short-term goals
- Offer guidance on finding your direction
- Assist with organizing and manifesting your own ideas
- Stimulate inspiration
- Help develop or enhance your leadership skills
- Motivate and empower

Take a moment to soak in that you have just taken a step towards transforming your management mindset!

Take charge of your kitchen!

In speaking with various female managers, I was amazed to discover just how many women were comfortable taking charge of their home, but weren't comfortable taking charge at work. Women must grow comfortable taking charge at work as though it were their own home. However, taking charge for example in your kitchen requires certain characteristics. Do you have the qualities it takes to be the leader?

GRAB YOUR APRON: BREAKING THROUGH STIGMAS

We may yearn for times of tremendous change for women in leadership, especially when it comes to the board room, but are women really prepared for such leadership? Abso-freakin-loutely! Many women feel unqualified to lead because they question their leadership skills and abilities, but I am here to help women help identify their leadership skills.

- The pressure on top managers has risen enormously. They need to deliver compelling results in less time. There is no room for weaknesses! The public image of top managers has degenerated into a cliché. While men often find it hard to admit their own limitations, women often are not offered the same leadership positions and have more practice with communicating these same limitations. The increase of women in top positions could bring a healthy turnaround from this point of view and encourage teamwork.

Head chef in charge: Women in leadership

Here, we will not address who is a better leader; male or female. We believe that both have the same capabilities but simply differ in the way they get the results. However, we will address the characteristics of female leadership.

- Multitasking- most women are phenomenal multitaskers. They are often in charge of a multitude of things and are expected to perform at a high level. In addition to household duties women are often tasked with maintaining a flourishing career, while also assisting with children's homework, grocery shopping, scheduling appointments, attending school functions, PTA meetings, and so on. I have learned that most women possess the skill to multitask several things at once, however, they tend to diminish and downplay their skills.

- Communication- many women excel at the art of thorough communication. We are often placed in positions where it is a requirement due to being ignored or our ideas are cast aside. Because of this many women have learned that in order to be heard; forward and concise communication is necessary for career growth.

As director of your company, being a good leader is important. It will allow you to have a motivated team with a sense of belonging and be more productive. Even with lower rates of financial problems, you will have a positive organizational climate and above all a high level of confidence, which will benefit you. You will be able to better delegate tasks, so that you focus on the business strategy.

The value of female leadership within companies is thought to be the democratic / participatory style that fosters relationships. The tendency of women in making decisions is to behave in a friendlier and empathetic way without leaving aside the interpersonal relationships of their team. In this way the role as a manager is more negotiating.

We know that there are different styles of leadership. You can be a combination of these when acting in certain situations that you face.

However, there is one that usually will always define you.

Considering the typical features of female leadership, we could say that women are characterized more by:

- ❖ **Empathy:**
  - ➢ *Taking into account feelings and expectations of her team to boost them professionally and make the best of them.*
- ❖ **Organization:**
  - ➢ *Having the ability to manage time efficiently by prioritizing tasks.*

> *Wanting to achieve concrete objectives and interaction between all the members of the team.*

- ❖ **Being direct:**
  > *Her feedback is based on results and achievement of objectives instead of criticism and punishment of non-compliance.*

- ❖ **Decision making:**
  > *Thinking about the best interests of the team.*

- *Getting involved in the projects that are under her direction and prefer to make consensus to reach the final decision.*
- *Share her "power" and information with her people, allowing for better decision making.*

❖ **Being maternal:**
- *Always seeking to reconcile and negotiate before attacking.*

❖ **Problem solving:**

- *Seeking alternatives to fix the issue at hand that will be most beneficial to the work needed while considering realistic expectations.*
- *Mixing intuition and rationality properly.*

❖ **Creativity:**
- *A feature especially in her way of taking command of her team. This allows her to be open to opinions, make collaborative*

groups, and be available to change.

Did you find any of these characteristics in the way you lead? If not, don't worry, exercising good leadership Is a matter of learning. Not everyone is born knowing how to be leaders, but we can become a person who is followed by his team with "closed eyes".

Mindset

It's critical to ensure balance and control when working with — or even just around — knives or hot pots and pans. It's also important to have a clear view of everything that's going on around you while you cook.

WEIGHING THE SCALES: WORK AND LIFE BALANCE

The balance between personal and work development remains a key issue in companies. It is essential to add activities that strengthen the links between employees and their families.

Explicitly expressing the difficulties of being a mother and professional is no easy feat. Although the participation of female staff in the business field is something already installed, organizations do not usually treat the issue instead they treat it as an everyday common place, where the behavior is unavoidable. While some women achieve a satisfactory balance between work and family by their own means, most of them need the support of their companies to try to achieve it. Therefore, it is essential to create activities that strengthen and favor links between employees and their families.

The woman of the 21st century seeks at all costs to have a balance in personal and professional life:

❖ *Why has it been so difficult to have a stable relationship and a united family?*

> *The 21st century gives us more technology that can*

assist with balancing work and home life.

❖ **Why is it so hard for us to enjoy our professional life?**

> ➢ *That's because schedules are from men to men, not for women who want to be with their children and work.*

Women often feel torn when it comes to their professional and personal goals. When facing the working world, she wants to be able to maintain all important relationships; her family, partner, children, boss, and her friends without sacrificing anything or anyone. The stress of making a perfect life without asking for favors or having a help network has been a conflict for many women.

This duality of seeking to be a woman and a mother or of being a mother and a woman is the one that worries the female world every day. Many see it as something separate instead of seeing it as an integral project of life, without sacrificing one role or another. Why is it so hard for us to set limits on the world of work and risk what we love most, which is our family? Why do we allow an entry schedule but do not set an exit schedule?

Work schedules are the reason many women have decided to set aside their career for a few years. In return, many women only seek job opportunities with flexible hours to work and be with their children. It is essential that women are able to seek out job opportunities that will allow them to be challenged in their professional career, not just because the schedule is more adaptable to work/life balance. In fixing this issue many women will be able to have their dream job and also be able to have a personal life. Fixing this work life balance issue for women will also benefit men. It will allow people that want to have more flexibility to spend time with their family with the opportunity. This way women don't feel like they are forced to pick between their professional career and starting a family.

Difference Between Tablespoon and Teaspoon: How to Achieve Balance

Faced with this issue, achieving a balance between professional and personal life is a continuous process. It requires time and effort to achieve it. Performing a review every time the activities are carried out daily will allow you room to build and/or adjust the harmony necessary to balance life and improve its quality. Life must have a balance between the professional and personal aspects. The wellbeing of the company and its employees are essential that this balance is able to be maintained.

Tips:

- ❖ **Organize those things that are a priority.**
  - ➢ *Although sometimes problems may arise that need to be resolved immediately, giving an order to the important things of each day will*

help to manage time more effectively.

- ❖ **Establish and respect the schedules with your activities.**
  - ➢ *The work schedule is regularly 8 hours and 1 or 2 hours of food as appropriate.*
  - ➢ *Comply with the time that should be devoted to the office.*
  - ➢ *Don't take work home or include work activities in the time allocated to the*

family and other personal issues or vice versa.

❖ **Schedule time to rest in daily activities.**

➢ *It is important that energy recharging activities be included in the agenda of the week.*

■ *Exercising, fun moments, meditating, reading, walking, and sleeping are good options.*

- **Allocate time for loved ones.**
  - *While it is true that the important thing is not the quantity but the quality of time, it is necessary to establish quantity with the family, children, and friends. In most cases they remain in the background for work activities.*

- **Rethink the activities.**
  - *Surely there will be things that are not so relevant.*

Things that are causing a waste of energy, investment of time, and disregard for oneself.

- *It is necessary to remove everything that is distracting and unusable for life.*

❖ **Set real goals.**

- *The thought of having a job and family makes you believe that the goals have been met, but both are just a part of a range of things that are required to achieve a balance in life. Therefore, setting goals and achieving the best results will be a cause of satisfaction and balance.*

- ❖ **Take care on the days off.**
  - ➢ *This time is for yourself, for loved ones, and those activities you want to carry out personally.*
    - ■ *Schedule a massage, go to*

therapy session, go shopping, get a makeover, go to the cinema, organize a party at home or outside with the family. Do what you need to do to unwind and reset. If you have children, organize activities to enjoy with them as well.

Creating a balance between family life and working life is one of the great challenges for organizations and women today. Both make up the triangle between family, business, and society and in turn build the wealth necessary for a company. You should think about policies that generate both business and personal responsibility to achieve the point of balance and survival.

Kie Ingredient 3

Pay attention to detail

Sugar and salt look the same but taste extremely different, the same can be said about paprika versus chili-powder?

WHAT! NO ONIONS? : STOP BEING THE VICTIM

No one said that working was easy. In fact, life is full of obstacles that we must overcome and the working world has tons. The key to the correct management of difficulties is in the attitude with which we face them. Even if you have a job you love, you will always have bad days that come along with problems to solve, such as co-workers you do not work well with, or perhaps a boss who willingly leaves you and your colleagues in despair. As trying as these things may have been, none of that justifies playing a victim as a defense mechanism.

Victimization is the tendency of an individual to consider themselves a victim or impersonate them. It becomes in most cases a way of life, since the person feels the need to hold others responsible for their problems. It is always much easier to be a "victim" of a situation, than to assume the responsibility that entails.

The "victim worker" greatly spreads the culture of the complaint throughout the organization. They are quick to address and spread their many misfortunes and "inappropriate behaviors" directed by others. The complaint is the manifestation of the feeling of one who never receives what they think they deserve. This attitude ends up creating a background of bitterness and disappointment. Not only for the one who manifests it, but also for the one who becomes a participant.

Victimization is the resource of the frightened. One who prefers to become an object of compassion, instead of facing a dilemma. On the other hand, such behavior can be adopted both consciously and unconsciously. Those who suffer victimization involuntarily live it as a parallel reality in which they are installed. They are not able to leave their own perception which destroys them little by little. Those who do it consciously, use it for their own benefit.

They are "simulated" victims, whose best weapons are manipulation and extraordinary handling of the feeling of guilt they throw on others.

There are definitely no onions: Victimization at work

We have all been victims at some point. While some (the majority) fight against the feeling of helplessness and have a hard time learning from experience, others choose to recreate themselves in self-pity.

An excellent phrase that portrays a victim mentality is:

"It is not my fault; everyone conspires against me and there is nothing I can do".

There are others that are also a classic. Let's see a small representation.

Victim behavior is characterized by:

- ❖ **The conversation focuses on their problems**

    - ➢ *The first thing that's obvious is that it reveals its drama story to the four winds. They will share it with everyone willing to listen. Usually to seek attention or to make others feel sorry, pity, and offer their help.*

- ❖ **They avoid taking responsibility for what happens by blaming others**
  - ➢ *The fault will always be of others, bad luck, or destiny. Never of their own actions.*

- ❖ **They react negatively**
  - ➢ *Becomes defensive if something sounds critical (even if it is constructive or advice).*

- **They think that the world conspires against them**
  - *To justify it, any trivial comment will turn into a personal attack. The same goes for any decision of the company. If they think it hurts them, they will say that they're disadvantaged by the machinations of other people.*
- **They exaggerate problems and exploit them to their advantage**
  - *A minor issue can be looked at as a major roadblock or a*

small difficulty. The victim only sees the situation as an insurmountable drama (or makes it happen as such). Which leads to the tendency to distort reality.

❖ **The successes of others are usually choked**

> *They prefer to attribute them to the preferential treatment that others have supposedly obtained instead of crediting hard work.*

Look, I found the onions! The reward the victimized pursues

Look at what you earn when victimized behavior works:

- ❖ *The attention of the environment, prominence*
- ❖ *The sympathy of others, their affection*
- ❖ *Pity and / or worry*
- ❖ *Belief of the right to special treatment*

All of this opens a world of possibilities to influence the thoughts, feelings, and actions of others. Because of the attention, sympathy, and confirmation that we have provided to the individual; the person with a victim's mentality achieves their purpose and obtains what they want. But not everything is profitable. Gradually the partners stop making plans with people who always seem to be angry, complaining or negative. They stop requesting or suggesting to work with these types in projects or group outings.

Do you suspect that you have a tendency to see things from a victim's perspective?

- **First, recognize yourself in that role.**
  - *Once identified, it is essential to want to get out of that situation by committing to make positive changes. The first of these changes is to take responsibility. Stop complaining and blaming others by accepting things as they come.*
- **The next step is to reflect.**

- *On the habits, thoughts, or beliefs that harm you and keep you in the role of victim. Once you know yourself better, work on the transformation of those habits and build others that help you feel more secure.*

❖ **Finally, it is essential to submit.**

- *The inner critical voice*
  - *not making up stories in your mind*

> *Take control of the situation and stop ruminating the problem try to think positively.*

If, on the contrary, the victimized is in your closest circle, it is best not to feed his drama or tolerate emotional blackmail. Set limits and don't let him use you. Be sure to keep in mind one thing: there are people who are a lost cause and little can be done to see things differently.

Kie Ingredient 4

Measure

The wiser you become (through more experience) the more you will be able to just eyeball, but everyone knows measurements make or break things. It's important that we measure ourselves in life and at work.

ASK FOR MOM'S RECIPE: SEEK WISDOM

The best long-term manager will be the one who acquires wisdom in human things and those of the company. However, no one speaks of wisdom in business schools or in the management manuals. Knowledge, leadership, data, intelligence, talent, and innovation are the buzzwords! The keys to the doors of success, the balm of Fierabrás that heals everything.

We work in the knowledge society. Companies compete for talent, we lead competent teams, and we revere the innovation that allows us to move forward. These are the concepts and capabilities that guide the ever-fluctuating fashions of business management and management techniques. But wisdom it seems, is neither expected nor unexpected. A great mistake that will be paid for by who forgets it.

Take Notes: Wisdom in Execution

Although the manager's wisdom involves reflection it is especially expressed in her actions, since she must guide her decisions and her way of leading. Therefore, the manager's wisdom even though sharing some common characteristics, has its own characteristics closely related to the company's own essence.

Depending on the reality in which she carries out her task, the wise manager, among other faculties is one who:

❖ **Makes clear what's for the staff and the company.**

> ➢ *Have projects, goals, and share the why of the company. Tell its mission and the value it brings to society. That vision will motivate you and serve as a compass in so many*

unknown areas that you will have to travel.

- ❖ **Deeply respects people and knows how to govern them.**
  - ➢ *Understand people's reasoning and motivations and anticipate their reactions. She knows her most important task. Knowing how to choose the right people and creating the climate so that they can work effectively in the service of an end shared by*

all. Delegates responsibilities functions and demands results from them. Her leadership directs everyone's work towards a common goal. She is comprehensive in personal matters, but demanding in results.

- ❖ **Knows how to decide intelligently.**
  - ➢ *She assumes responsibility and risk always after a thoughtful analysis of pros*

and cons. She knows the measures of risks and knows which one is worth running and which one is not.

- *She needs some boldness, but intelligent boldness never blind or self-sufficient.*
- *Prioritize decisions, know how to distinguish between important and urgent ones. We are above all, what we decide. The right decision is the fundamental engine of the successful company.*

❖ **Knows how to listen and be open to critical learning.**

> *She must contrast the opinion of the market, customers, suppliers, equipment, workers, and consultants. Only the fool is surrounded by flatterers. The wise seek the contrast of opinions, although sometimes they may be opposed.*

> *She knows how to manage her pride and learns to*

rectify. Therefore, she also questions herself and is open to change if reality shows her mistake.

- ❖ **Demands the ethical behavior of the company and its managers.**

  - ➢ *She bases her leadership on her own expertise, knowing the meanings and ways of her works.*

  - ➢ *Actions speak louder than words, lead by example. She knows there are no shortcuts and expects the same actions from the company and its managers.*

- ❖ **Combines strategic thinking with tactical ability.**
  - ➤ *She knows how to rise from the concrete complex situation, raise her gaze, and overcome the passions to acquire the right perspective. The person who sees beyond others is wise.*

- *Who is able to understand the sign of the times?*
- *Who anticipates trends and guides the company in their favor?*

We manage as we are. So, if we want to manage better, we will have to become better people. The wise manager must not only be in continuous learning, but must also cultivate.

- *The strategic vision implies the correct reading of the*

circumstances in which the company will operate in its social, political, economical, and technological dimension. She knows that reality, circumstances, and society change.

❖ **Know your business perfectly, the strengths and weaknesses of your services or products.**

> *She knows where she wins and where she loses. Listen to technical managers and discuss*

with them until you understand the essence of the business.

➢ Strive for the best management and permanent improvement in quality, image, and costs. Achieving it in the best possible way is a priority objective of the wise manager.

➢ She is aware that the company is sustained and growing thanks to its *benefits. She prefers sustained long-term benefits than rushing because of uncertainties for the future. It requires strict budgetary, financial and cost control to always know where it is.*

- ❖ **Knows how to use the energy of conflicts.**

  - ➢ *The conflict generates a great energy that can destroy you. If you know how to channel it and take advantage of it, it can't catapult you. Therefore, it's the essence of opportunity.*

> *She knows how to listen and negotiate and strives to improve her effective communication skills.*

❖ **She knows that she is not only valued for her management but for her ability to represent the company and its values.**

> *She cultivates her social talents, in relation to*

others, as well as her political talents.

- *She understands the relationship of internal and external powers.*
- *She knows that the image of the company and the values that evoke her signature and her products are fundamental.*

❖ **The wise manager knows others.**

- *She knows the competition, the regulators and her own team.*
- *Above all, and this is the most difficult thing, she must learn herself. We manage as we are, so if we want to manage better we will have to become better people. The wise manager must not only be in continuous learning, but must also cultivate in*

a path of personal development that leads her to wisdom.

It can be achieved. We all know the example of wise managers who enlighten us. Let us reflect and apply ourselves in the matter. As García Márquez wrote, "wisdom comes to us when it no longer serves us".

Kie Ingredient 5

Be prepared to make a disastrous meal!!

Some recipes can take years to perfect, and must be frequently fine-tuned. It is imperative that you understand that it takes practice and multiple attempts.

Don't Stain The Pots and Pans: Self-Discipline & Productivity

I have always been a very disciplined person. It's what makes me feel powerful and confident. The main obstacle of those struggling to improve their productivity is not only summarized by a lack of understanding or learning, but rather an absence of self-discipline. There are many who flood the network with tips, tricks, and systems on productivity and get more in less time. However, many have problems to implement these tools despite having a clear purpose.

Strength training makes the muscle stronger!

The power to act on ideas, extract things from thoughts, and make them happen through actions to achieve tangible results. This is self-discipline! Self-discipline is like a muscle. It gets stronger the more you work on it. Therefore, to have self-discipline from the point of view of productivity is to be motivated and to be able to do something.

Knowledge is only part of the path. Knowing about productivity does not mean being more productive or being more efficient. It is a necessary step obviously, but what makes the difference is the implementation. If you do not take action then the time and effort devoted to learning will not be worth it.

Having said that, let's go back to the muscle and why the comparison. What happens when you can't lift the heaviest weights in the gym? You lose motivation and every time you try; it feels heavier. The most sensible thing will be to start with the small conquests and exercise your muscles. The key is in the small changes. Small successes will prepare you for futures in the following stages.

The same thing happens with self-discipline. From the beginning, you try to face the big problems of your life, yet you fail again and again. The problems are too big for you to overcome. Little by little the force of self-discipline will increase and with greater momentum you can face major problems and changes. Don't pretend a muscle is strong and developed if it isn't. Especially if you have allowed your muscle to atrophy and bad habits have taken over you.

Set your target for maximum productivity!

Self-discipline is the affirmation of the will on the most basic desires. It is generally understood as a synonym for "self-control." It is also to some extent a substitute for motivation. No matter what rejections you have, they are part of the process. Being productive is not necessarily being bright. It has a lot to do with being disciplined enough to sit and work on what you want. I think the trick to being disciplined is to convince yourself that you are the one who wants to succeed. If you really want something, don't see it as a sacrifice to have to work to achieve it.

Your thoughts go through a negative battlefield which makes you block and cloud your goals. Therefore, blocking your productivity. This is where self-sabotage begins. You don't need much to get there, just a hint of lack of trust. When you use your thoughts to focus properly, you will have less stress and feel more secure. Each person has the key to become what one wants. Focus. Concentrate on doing the best you can and not get carried away by negativity. Overcome these fears and negative thoughts to move forward.

Be clear about what you like and the paths you can follow or not. Not having a plan or route to follow will make you unproductive. It is also important to be realistic with yourself. Know the limitations and what you want to achieve. Train yourself and ask for help whenever you need it, without repairs of any kind. Do not put limits on your productivity out of fear of failure. Concentrate, focus and then do.

Discover the greatness that is in you!

If you are not able to develop the ability to discipline yourself, you will never achieve such greatness. All this potential you have will remain locked in you and die with you. So, a day will come when you will regret it. If you are able to be disciplined, your behavior will change and you will feel completely unlimited. Everything that goes through your imagination can be turned into reality.

To see the fruits of your greatness, you just need to know that:

- ❖ *It is something you must work on "manually."*
  - ➢ *It will not appear automatically.*
- ❖ *The feeling of inadequacy, or as though you don't belong, immediately begins to dissipate once you begin yielding fruit.*

You are your own leader. Only you have the ability to discipline yourself to achieve success and do something you always wanted to do.

Imagine a ship in the middle of the ocean. The crew is dedicated to fulfilling their duties but there is no captain to guide them. The only thing left to do is roam the ocean without a fixed direction. Like this ship, you need a captain, and there is no one better than you to take charge of your ship. For a good address, you will need a plan and execute it.

Choose a specific task to do for 6 or 7 days a week, for 1 month. A task that you know will improve your life. If you start up the task and there comes a time when you want to throw in the towel, remember not to listen to that little inner voice. Your intelligence will be against you. You will have to block it and trust your leadership. Remember that breaking a promise is giving up on oneself. Also giving up on your greatness. To be disciplined is to create a very powerful connection between what you want to do and what you really execute. If you get it during that month, you will have control over yourself and will be prepared to take on another activity of even greater difficulty.

Self confidence

We have all had a fight with ourselves and lacked confidence. We have all not liked things we have done. We have been rejected or things may have not gone as planned. We forget the times where we have done things well and the awards. We have forgotten how happy we were while working hard on what we wanted. Just remembering that feeling of happiness already leads to greater and better productivity. This together with self-esteem and being convinced of the quality of your work, no matter what others think, are key to being disciplined.

It is necessary to be able to control yourself and not be manipulated by negative feelings. Be patient and persistent. Keep a clear vision about your current situation to create a decision and continue with perseverance until you achieve the success you pursue. All of this is willpower and hard work. Just don't forget to give yourself some respite from time to time. Give yourself permission to relax. Enjoy life doing all those activities that you also like to do.

Part II: 6-12

Kie Ingredient 6

Preparation

Preparing to do the great things that you want to do.

Planning and Organization of Time

Recipe Building: The importance of planning

Planning allows combining activities and people with different occupations. Matching over time is key to moving forward without wasting time in the organization. Planning is essential because it describes the route, we will all follow in a project. Making sure no one is left behind or goes out of the way. We objectify the steps we have to take, the deadlines, and the content. If we are realistic with the planning, we will achieve the results.

We also have to plan our work in a way that is digestible. We have to keep in mind that each task requires a different energy and skills. Therefore, when we prepare to plan the tasks, we will have to intelligently distribute in time what we have to do. We have to start at our least attractive to find ourselves in the best physical and mental conditions. The fresher we are the better we will think. There are tasks that have to be undertaken alone, while others will be developed collectively.

Planning should not, nor can, take too much time. It would be a contradiction in itself. We have to plan for small units that once aligned would make up extensive planning. Point out what we have to achieve today, this week, this month, and so on. So, step by step we specify the results.

Serving Size: Optimization of the agenda

We must have an agenda, both conceptually and physically. It doesn't matter if it's paper or electronic. The important thing is to have a space where we write down what we have to do, the place, the day and the time. Then we have to overcome laziness and aim to read it. Acquiring the habit of reviewing every day what we have to do the next day will give us control over time management. It will also prevent us from avoiding commitments.

It is not enough to write down meetings or events that arise. It is very important to add the related details such as the place or the possible related people. It is key to consider these when calculating transfers to optimize them and anticipate how we will perform them, etc. Many lack punctuality in meetings of all kinds. This is a consequence of the lack of forecast in the time interval between one activity and the next.

When we have events that are repeated periodically it will be very timely to leave it pointed over time. In this way, we avoid surprises and protect those commitments. With programs on computers and digital agendas it is now easy to schedule the repetition of these meetings and periodic tasks. Set alerts or alarms programmed in advance. We want to ensure that an appointment will not fall into oblivion. Depending on the nature of the meeting, we will be interested in being alerted five minutes in advance or several days in advance.

We apply all of the above to meetings and interviews, but we can also transfer it to specific tasks that we have to perform. One of these typical tasks is phone calls or sending messages by mobile or email. When we do not systematize the multitude of tasks, we run the risk of accumulation. Some pass from one day to the next with the disastrous consequences of lack of productivity.

Collect the ingredients: Programming towards obtaining results

Only with clear objectives will we be able to schedule the activities that bring us closer to the goal. The objective draws a line in time. This is what we call a schedule. We are placing the different phases and actions of the project in its strict or broader sense. The important thing is to have a map of where we want to go and try to follow it faithfully.

Two basic actions will help us to program well:

❖ Prioritize over time

> *That is what we have to do first so that a second phase, a third phase, and a fourth phase can be initiated. It is not a priority because of the value of the activity itself, but because*

of the strategic position it occupies throughout the process. It is aimed at preventing collapse and funnel effects that are so often repeated in organizations.

- ❖ **Place in time the beginning and end of each activity**
  - ➢ *Beginning and end. Both dates are essential; It is what we know as deadlines. Leaving it for when the time comes is an*

error of irreparable consequences.

- ■ *Serve the example of a puzzle, without all the pieces we will never finish the puzzle.*
- ➢ *Set objectives, establish phases in time, review compliance with intermediate dates, and take appropriate measures to readjust. The programming system itself*

forces time management in an efficient and intelligent way.

Consequence of all of the above is the need to plan. There is no organization that is not planned. They are all valid if they are consistent with what they pursue. Without planning we will go aimlessly. Even if we move forward it will be difficult to know if the route was the most effective and profitable.

Kie Ingredient 7

Cooking

Stepping into your enhancement kitchen (transition from thinking and planning to putting it into action)

Follow The Recipe: Self-Leadership & Construction of the Leader

Self-leadership is essential for the development of a person in any area of her life, not only in the professional field. It is essential that a leader (someone who has the responsibility of leading others), previously develops this ability. Self-leadership implies a deep knowledge of oneself. It has its starting point, the questioning approach, and the search for solutions. In the process of building self-leadership you can make mistakes, but you also have the opportunity to overcome and learn from them.

Therefore, control over our own emotions is required. This way you won't be blinded by success or feel overwhelmed by failure.

The leader is someone who continuously learns and demonstrates humility in the face of new knowledge. This form of self-control is sharpened through leadership styles. Not all organizations are equal and in work teams. That's why it is necessary for a leader to develop a style. One that helps to enhance the characteristics of their team, consider the type of tasks they perform, and the organization in which they are located.

A leader develops an idea, sets goals, communicates them to the members of their team, and makes them participate in achieving them. A leader is able to inspire their team and convince them of the path they must take to meet goals. The leader, as Warren Bennis said, "transforms the vision into reality". If you don't previously forge those convictions and push towards yourself, you probably won't succeed in inspiring others.

Kie Ingredient 8

Tidy yourself and cooking area

When it is time to cook, it is also time to clean.

THE PERCEPTION IN THE WORK AREA

Perception in the work area is very important. Although we are not aware, perceptions can influence our day to day work. In order to better understand this term, which is very influential in our work area, we are going to investigate its meaning in depth.

Wash Hands: What Is Perception?

"There is nothing we know that does not come from the perception of the senses; of the understanding of the

soul and the understanding of the mind" -Aristotle

Our senses provide us with data from the unprocessed outside world. This data has no meaning. So, an interpretation process is required to find a relationship with us. From this moment the perception enters the game.

Declutter to Create Room: Perception Processes

❖ **First process**:

> ➢ *Selection of all the information acquired from the outside*
>
> ➢ *Reducing complexity*

> *Making easy storage in our memory.*

❖ **Second process:**

> *An attempt to know future events so surprises are reduced.*

This makes us understand that by perceiving a person or an object, we create an order of everything we acquire. This order allows us to verify the information, in order to add more information of interest to ourselves. We will be able to perceive behaviors and situations that occur around us.

Through the perceptual process we are able to transform, or alter reality by adding information that does not come with the stimulus. This information can create negative thoughts which are generated by an uncertainty. This happens when we face a situation whose meaning is not clear. It consequently creates doubt and insecurity. These negative thoughts have important effects on the individual and can start a labor dispute.

Clean up Emotionally, Physically, and Spiritually for Enhancement: Handling Conflict

Conflict is the action or thought that works in the opposite way between two or more people. We can argue that different perceptions can generate an action or thought, contrary to another person known as labor conflict.

The reason for the difference in perception is generated by different aspects such as:

❖ *Personal interests*

- *A bad integration in the work area*
- *Inequality in the distribution of resources*
- *Ambition for power*
- *Difference between personal and / or group goals*

The effect of the conflict in the organization is varied. Perception in the work area and conflict can establish a healthy situation of demand when allocating resources. Or it can be an insurmountable barrier to the achievement of goals.

You Can't Cook in A Filthy Kitchen: Importance of Perception in The Work Area

Changing employees' perception of their place within a company is sometimes a complicated yet effective way to improve the work environment and avoid conflicts. Employees who perceive that they have greater control over their working life will probably be more motivated to excel within the organizational structure. In organizations, conflict and stress are common. Perception is the process that mediates between situations and these two effects. Whether or not a stimulus causes stress depends largely on the perception of the individual exposed to it.

Being able to understand the perceptual process can be of importance. It can give us clues about specific problems that can be found in the work area. Knowing the elements that influence the formation of the perception of individuals within our company, allows us to attend them properly.

Kie Ingredient 9

Keep a close eye on what your cooking

We have to keep a watchful eye on the things that we are building in life.

AVOIDING TOXIC WORK ENVIRONMENTS

As women we need passion, encouragement, support, and all the good that may exist. However, the reality is different. In many cases the environment only discourages us, helps us to be undisciplined, and blurs us from our vision.

Toxic work environment is known as a work environment that is marked by personal problems among its different members. Where drama, fights, and other conflicts interfere with employee productivity. They generally produce negative consequences amongst the people who are involved.

These types of work environments are usually generated because of the presence of toxic people; Individuals who seek personal gain (such as power, money, fame or a specific status) regardless of what they have to do to get it.

The topic of toxic work environments is increasingly studied in all types of environments. It is believed that it may be at the base of very serious problems at work. For example, several investigations suggest that this type of environment can be one of the main causes of workplace harassment or violence in the company. In this chapter we will see the main characteristics of a toxic work environment. As well as the most common consequences that occur and what an individual can do to avoid the worst of them.

Adjust the Fire and Stir to Keep from Burning: Characteristics of a Toxic Work Environment

Workers avoid attracting attention

The first symptom of a toxic work environment is the presence in which punishments abound. Workers immersed in such a situation quickly learn that if they stand out in some way (for example, making a suggestion, criticism, or making a mistake), they will be attacked or punished. The feeling employees have in this type of environment is that they should simply shut up and continue working without asking questions. This generally leads to problems such as demotivation, lack of creativity, and increased stress since workers never know when they will receive the next punishment.

Bad communication

Another of the most important characteristics of a toxic work environment is a constant lack of communication. It prevents workers from improving and knowing exactly what they have to do. Normally, the feedback they receive is non-existent with the exception of the previously mentioned criticisms. In these work environments employees usually do not feel heard at all. In the most serious cases, bosses or even other workers may claim credit for what other people have done. This is one of the clearest signs of a toxic work environment.

Negative attitudes

Going to work day after day may not be the most motivating activity in the world. When all employees are sad, stressed, or angry there is more than likely a certain level of toxicity in the work environment. In more severe cases, it is common to see more and more workers begin to develop symptoms of emotional problems, such as burnout syndrome or depression. It is not uncommon for the number of casualties to increase, and for employees to present their resignation to escape the toxic environment.

Presence of constant drama

A toxic work environment can in many ways resemble an institute class. Instead of focusing on their tasks, employees who favor the creation of this environment are dedicated to criticizing others, spreading rumors and insanely encouraging competition. This usually results in fights, misunderstandings, and conflicts between different workers. Due to this, employees spend more time arguing with each other, looking for allies, and complaining about their peers than actually attending to their tasks.

Difficulty getting results

In a toxic work environment, none of the company's objectives seem to be adequately met. Workers are not entirely clear about what they should do, and bosses are more concerned with their own problems than with providing clear leadership. In these environments, team meetings are usually useless. Instead of proposing solutions and developing action plans, conflicts and personal wars appear. In addition, it is also common to constantly add new rules and regulations that add even more confusion to the environment.

Lack of concern for the welfare of workers

Finally, in a toxic work environment problems and concerns of workers are not taken into account. The only thing that matters is to achieve the objectives of the bosses or the company. Therefore, employees are expected to sacrifice their well-being and personal life for the good of their company.

Some of the most obvious symptoms of this feature are the absence of vacations, the requirement that workers make "overtime" unpaid, or the need to be on the phone 24 hours in case an emergency arises. If an employee decides to stick to the tasks specified in his contract, both their bosses and colleagues will pressure them to work harder. Fierce competitiveness usually appears amongst the members of the company, and empathy between them disappears completely.

You Can't Open the Oven for Certain Foods: Consequences

No motivation

Employees who are immersed in a toxic work environment often report feeling unmotivated and lack energy to perform their tasks. The impediments with which they find themselves to carry out their tasks, along with the constant drama and conflict between workers usually make a dent in the mood of even the most resistant workers.

Therefore, productivity in the company tends to decrease. Workers feel less involved with their responsibilities, and only make the minimum effort required to avoid problems with their superiors. This reinforces the shortfall of motivation in a negative spiral that is very difficult to break.

Shortage of results

When both bosses and workers are more concerned with their own personal problems than with the company's objectives, it becomes increasingly difficult to achieve the desired results. Depending on the type of company, the results can be more or less serious. If the toxic work environment occurs in a small part of a large company, the main problem will be the discomfort felt by workers who are immersed in it. On the contrary, for a business that is not too big or is just beginning, these difficulties can mean the appearance of very serious economic problems.

Workplace harassment and violence

Several studies suggest that the presence of a toxic work environment could be at the base of more serious problems. Problems such as workplace harassment (also known as mobbing) and violence in the workplace. When one of these environments occur, competitiveness increases exponentially. Some workers will not hesitate to use whatever method is necessary to stand out from others. In the most extreme cases, they will try to cheerfully destroy their competitors, or even resort to physical threats. The work environment then becomes a battlefield, which worsens all other consequences and negatively affects the welfare of employees.

Generation of personal problems

Perhaps the most worrisome consequence of a toxic work environment is the appearance of problems that affect employees not only in their job, but also in their personal lives. Being immersed in this type of environment can seriously damage someone's psychological well-being in different ways. The most common consequence of this type is chronic stress, also known as burnout. People who suffer from it feel a lack of energy, loss of interest, and their health suffers. In general, their mood worsens. In serious cases, long term in a toxic work environment can lead to more serious psychological problems. The two most common are anxiety and depression. These are the most mentioned reasons for requesting a leave.

Avoid Burns: How to avoid it?

Making a toxic work environment disappear completely can be extremely complicated. It often does not depend on one single person, but on all of those who are immersed in it. It is not usually realistic to expect all problems to be solved. However, the latest research suggests that it is possible to avoid the most negative consequences produced by these types of environments individually.

Following the actions below can help alleviate harmful effects, such as:

- *Distancing yourself from the most toxic people*
- *Practicing relaxation*
- *Cognitive therapy*

On many occasions it may be necessary to consider the possibility of leaving a toxic work environment and looking for a new job. Finding a new job can be complicated, but when our physical and mental health are at stake, it is often not worth continuing long in a harmful environment.

> Kie Ingredient 10

Gathering your seasonings

It's important to know your seasonings. These different seasonings can attribute many flavors to your dish.

Core Seasonings for every dish:

- A pinch of passion
- A dash of determination
- A sprinkle of strength
- A dab of drive
- A smidge of self-discipline
- A teaspoon of thorough thoughts
- A cup of capability
- An ounce of obedience
- A pound of problem solving

Personality Attributes & Organizational Behavior

Personality is the way in which an individual reacts to others and interacts with them. Here we will expose the main personality attributes that influence organizational behavior. Various personality attributes can help predict behavior in organizations.

These attributes are:

❖ **Locus of control:**

> *In 1954 Julian B. Rotter developed a concept on Locus of Control. The concept was divided into two*

categories, internal and external. If an individual had possessed and internal locus of control, then the person attributes his/her success to his/her efforts. If an individual possesses an external locus of control, which is someone who attributes his/her achievement to luck or destiny, is less likely to make the contributions needed to advance and learn.

➢ *In general terms, research and evidence indicated that individuals who possessed an internal locus performed better in his/her work. They typically sought information more actively before making a decision, were more motivated for achievement, had more initiative, and attempted to more actively control his or her environment. Unlike those who possessed an external locus, who tend to be more submissive and await instructions to proceed to act. People with an external locus of control were more likely to experience anxiety because they honestly believed that they were not in control of their own lives. They do not feel very motivated and present greater absenteeism.*

❖ Achievement orientation:

> *This is considered a personality characteristic that varies between people and can be used to predict certain behaviors. Those who have a dying need for achievement are people who struggle to make things better. They want to overcome obstacles and don't give up easily. Yet, they also want to feel that success (or failure) is due to their own actions.*

> *These people like to take on tasks of intermediate difficulty. They are not interested in easy tasks because they want to test their ability, but they also avoid very difficult tasks because of little probability of success. They have a great motivation for achievement. They're more likely to take on tasks where the results are directly attributable to their*

efforts. Consequently, looking for challenges with a probability of success of approximately 50-50.

- ❖ **Authoritarianism:**
  - ➢ *Describes the extremely authoritarian person as one who shows intellectual rigidity, judges others, and seek to please superiors. They exploit subordinates, distrusts, and is resistant to change.*

➤ *Certainly, there are few people being extremely authoritarian. However, it should be noted that whoever has a very authoritarian personality will not be able to perform positively in positions that require sensitivity to the feelings of others, and ability to adapt to changes. On the contrary, they will perform well in highly structured jobs where success depends on submitting to rules and norms without discussion.*

Machiavellianism:

- *This attribute is closely related to authoritarianism. Whoever has this characteristic to a high degree is usually pragmatic, maintains emotional distance, and is convinced that the end justifies the means. The important thing is that the expected result is given.*

- *The "Machiavellians" are individuals who manipulate, earn more, and are more difficult to persuade. They usually have greater convincing power than people who are not Machiavellian.*
- *Various studies indicate that Machiavellians thrive by interacting directly*

instead of indirectly when the situation has few rules and norms which allows them to improvise.

❖ Acceptance of risks:

> *People have different degrees of taking risks. The propensity to take risks or avoid them influences the time it takes for managers to make decisions and the amount of information they need to do so. Those who are more willing to take*

risks tend to make decisions faster than those who are less prone to risk.

- *The risk propensity can favor a better performance in the case of a stockbroker, whose job is precisely to make decisions quickly. On the other hand, those with the lowest risk propensity would perform better in a firm that performs audit activities.*

Kie Ingredient 11

Setting the table

Figure out your placement, check your setup, and Choose your centerpiece. This should be the paste that holds everything together.

HOW TO LEAD A HIGH-PERFORMANCE TEAM

Every leader poses a key question:

How do I achieve maximum performance from my team?

Part of the answer to the question is in the efficient use of management tools. It is also the knowledge of the different personalities that make up the team and how to use them. A high-performance team is not a simple work group, much less the sum of individuals that fulfill their specific tasks in isolation. In that sense, there is a clear difference or evolution from the concept of the collection of individuals to the high-performance team.

A big difference between high performance teams and the rest of the work teams is that leadership can be shared there. For this reason, its members must also develop competencies and skills related to business management and must be able to behave as leaders if the situation requires it.

Seat Your Guests: The team

Knowing each member allows the leader to clearly identify the competences of each one and establish the necessary synergies within the team to achieve the objectives. The knowledge of the group helps to know what the competences are at the collective level. The knowledge of the organization provides a compression of the general processes of the organizational climate and other characteristics that constitute its seal.

A fundamental characteristic of a high-performance team is the fluidity in communication. It allows the establishment of clear goals, their transmission, the generation of trust, and the high level of involvement of the members.

In the high-performance teams, tools for problem solving and process visualization are also used. As well as, people management tools such as coaching, which identify the root of performance problems and involve the person in their solution.

As a result, a work environment is achieved with full participation of the team members. Not only in the execution of tasks, but also in decision making.

Make Sure Everything Is Put Together Correctly: Recruitment and Skills Training

Companies have traditionally recruited based on criteria such as knowledge or level of intelligence, but the workers don't always give the expected results. Other factors must be considered today. In the traditional processes of evaluation of applicants, the need to acquire new knowledge, emotional management, and relationships with other people have also been considered.

Among the new elements to be taken into account when recruiting, companies especially consider the competencies required to fulfill the functions. It so happens that the classic evaluation criteria when hiring does not guarantee the selected worker efficiently fulfills their duties, nor that the selected training process helps in that regard.

A fundamental question then arises:

What characteristics must a worker meet in order to be efficient?

Your Centerpiece Should Represent You and Your Work: Competencies beyond knowledge

Competence is a more complex and complete characteristic of a person. It's not only "knowledge" but also technical and interpersonal skills. Each person can develop different competencies. Each job may require some very specific ones, that will allow the worker who possesses them to be able to efficiently perform their duties. Once competencies are identified it can enhance the performance of a worker.

Many companies invest in hiring and training personnel to work as a team, when jobs probably require a higher level of introspection and concentration. This results in a low level of collaboration.

McClelland conducted experiments at the beginning of the 1970s in which he showed that the workers with the best performance in a given position were not necessarily the most intelligent or had the most knowledge. It was actually those who had managed to develop some specific skills that were very useful for the job. Proper identification of these skills can help develop training programs focused on their development.

Kie Ingredient 12

Pay attention to the recipe

Some things require constant supervision while others require none. Taste test along the way, not just the final product.

Employee Engagement

Dedicated employees not only do their job particularly well, but also promote teamwork and a good working atmosphere. Dedicated employees are an essential prerequisite for a company to function. They think! They do not just wait for instructions, they get involved. They take responsibility and care about the well-being of the whole company. However, not all employees are equally committed. Even in the same department there can be particularly committed colleagues, while others fulfill their tasks only as necessary.

Executives are happy to have committed employees because they relieve them of their work and support them. They need minimal explanation and you do not always have to check how far they have come. Supervisors can easily rely on these employees. Even if they sometimes overshoot their goals.

How Will Guests Receive This Meal?: Motivation for a specific task

Leaders want to know how to promote employee engagement among their employees because it is generally beneficial to the business.

Employee engagement generally refers to the extent to which an employee contributes to their work and tasks. They invest physical energy, make many thoughts, and have positive feelings for their work. It is crucial that they really do what is visible and not have an attitude as they work. To measure the level of engagement, scientists have developed different measurement systems. These often consist of specific statements for which the employees should make an assessment on a scale to what extent they would make the respective statement about themselves.

In the evaluation sheets, statements are for example as follows:

❖ *When I'm working, time flies by.*

- ❖ *I think that my work is a positive challenge for me.*
- ❖ *I always find new and interesting aspects in my work.*
- ❖ *I invest a lot of personal energy in my work.*
- ❖ *I feel strong and powerful in my work.*
- ❖ *I have the feeling that I think fast with my work.*

This makes visible what employee engagement is all about. It is difficult to make tangible, although it is somehow visible to all. They have developed the following model and evaluated numerous studies. In doing so, they want to find out which factors are particularly conducive to engagement and which ones are less or not at all.

Many different factors divide into three categories:

Characteristics of the workplace and work organization:

- ❖ *Autonomy*
- ❖ *Variety of tasks*
- ❖ *Feedback*
- ❖ *Working conditions in general*

Characteristics of leadership:

- *The ability to work on new tasks*
- *The ability to solve problems*
- *Support from others*

Behavior and leadership style of the supervisor personal characteristics:

- *Attentive and conscientious*
- *Positive attitude to life and work*
- *To be generally engaged and interested.*

I identified some of the most conducive factors for employee engagement.

Most important are:

- *The work is varied. The employee may have to or must do different things:*
    - *Calculate*
    - *Check*
    - *Edit*
    - *Write*
    - *Discuss*
    - *etc.*
- *The employee knows why their work and the respective task are*

important. They recognize the superordinate connections. The goals and strategies for which their activity is significant. They see the meaning of their work.

- *Personal traits also play a big role. Some people are naturally interested, curious, active, helpful, conscientious, reliable and committed - no matter what. Dedicated people are also more extroverted. They approach people who are sociable and have many social and emotional skills.*

Remember Serve From The Left: The superiors are less important

Surprisingly, it hardly plays a role for dedicated people, which leadership style the boss maintains. No matter the freedom they allow, whether they provide regular feedback, or if they are inspiring. No matter if their inspirational, or simply gives directions. It is not so important to employees when it comes to engagement or not.

After all, some studies attach importance to the relationship between employees and their supervisor.

It is important that the supervisor shows the following behavior:

- *She makes clear statements*
- *She is fair*
- *She sees good performances and expresses her appreciation **(praise!)***

Thus, the employee realizes that they can trust their supervisor and they can rely on her statements. This creates security, which is an important prerequisite for her commitment. In addition, the supervisor always plays an important role when it comes to convey the meaning of the task and to show the connections:

- ❖ *To which higher-level processes does the task belong?*
- ❖ *Which strategies are pursued?*
- ❖ *What corporate goals are achieved?*
- ❖ *How can it be used to meet customer requirements?*
  - ➢ *This must make the manager visible.*

It is also very important that the requirements a boss places on her employees match their competencies. Anyone who feels overwhelmed or under-challenged may slow down in commitment. The same applies to the personal needs of an employee and the rewards they receive. Both must match as well. There is something management can do, and that's hire the right people. Since their attitude towards work and colleagues is particularly important, conscientious, active, and positive thinking employees should be preferred.

Many analysis and employee surveys only check whether the employees are satisfied with their job. Even if employees say "yes," that does not mean they are engaging in their work in a special way. Both must be separated. Commitment is always tied to the individual task. If this is varied and if it makes sense to the performer, then she gets involved. Anyone who is open, open-minded, positive, curious, conscientious and reliable about her personality will do so even more.

Managers can contribute little to this. They should make clear, reliable statements or give instructions. They should be fair and sometimes praise. Then the employees feel confirmed and on the safe side. They then dare and bring in more. That's important to the whole company.

A dedicated employee does his job much more efficiently and effectively. They also create an environment that promotes teamwork, where colleagues help and coordinate with each other. That helps make the organization work better overall.

Collect from The Right: How Do You Motivate Your Employees?

Autonomy

Employees perform best when they can work on their own responsibility. This also means being able to determine flexible working hours. When, where, and how the work is done. Regardless of role or position, there are usually opportunities to increase personal responsibility for the individual. In some areas, it may be sufficient to give control over how to focus attention on the measurable results. Where this is not possible small changes such as, permission to organize and equip sections at their own discretion can be an important step in the right direction.

Development

Employees need the opportunity to develop and improve their existing skills as they work and acquire new skills. This does not necessarily mean having to invest regularly in training. Rather, it is about discussing with each employee professional ambitions, expectations, and interests and aligning them with business. Having a mentoring program with experienced colleagues or temporarily gaining experience at other sites may be enough to make your employees feel they can move forward.

Membership

Understanding why you do something helps to pursue your goal. Affiliation is the feeling of being involved in a large, meaningful whole. For the company, that means sharing goals and visions with employees, not just sales.

Motivation

Motivation is essential for employee engagement, dedication, satisfaction, and performance. Low motivation leads to low commitment, increased absenteeism, and general restraint of your employees. It is important to understand the lack of commitment and demotivation as well as their cause. It is important to recognize every single employee with their individual motivators. For example, some are motivated by external factors and need clear guidelines and incentives to do their best. In turn, intrinsically motivated workers have their own motivational factors that leaders should recognize and support.

To motivate employees in the workplace depends essentially on perceiving each individual as an individual. It is important to recognize the individual wishes of the individual employees for development and development opportunities and to create the corresponding structures that offer these possibilities. Use our tools to find out what motivates your employees. Your tools will also help you take the appropriate steps to achieve a high level of employee engagement.

Stay on Task: How to Hold Your Employees Accountable

Here are some practical ways you can increase accountability on your team:

- ❖ **Set goals and clear expectations**
    - ➢ *It's hard to hold someone accountable to a standard that hasn't been set. Create clear goals and expectations in the form of performance plans, or an employee handbook that outlines rules*

and guidelines for employee behavior. Once goals and expectations have been established, communicate them clearly and put them in writing. Having your expectations in writing such as an email or handbook will allow you to easily reference the conversation if an employee fails to deliver on expectations.

- ❖ **Understand how your employees are wired.**

➢ *Set clear expectations, then follow up with your staff members to ensure that what you communicated was fully understood. One of the largest issues that causes the most destruction in an organization, is miscommunication.*

➢ *Using the results of a talent optimization tool such as the PI Behavioral Assessment, you can learn how your employees are wired to receive information. For example, if they have a high drive, they might need some time to talk it out and make sure they are understanding what is being asked of them. If your employee has a high formality drive, they may need detailed instructions to ensure that they know which process to follow when executing a task.*

❖ **_Be prepared to give feedback._**

- *You will at some point need to hold someone accountable. This is simply a part of people management. The good news is employees want your feedback. They want to know what they are doing right and what needs improvement.*
- *When giving feedback, focus on the behavior and not the employee. Be specific, offer corrective action and let them know the*

consequences of the continuing said behavior.

Here's an example:

"John, our company policy is that employees must arrive for work by 9 a.m. You arrived at 9:10 last Tuesday, 9:15 on Monday, and 9:05 today. I need you to arrive at or before 9 a.m. if you continue to be late to work, I'm afraid

we'll have to loop HR into our conversation."

(This is, of course, assuming that there are no legally valid, extenuating circumstances for being late.)

❖ **Stay on top of it.**

> *Pay attention to what your employees are doing and whether they're upholding the standards you set.*

While most managers are working double-time, performing their job duties, and managing direct reports, management can't take a backseat. To ensure consistency in holding employees accountable and catching something sooner rather than later, stay on top of what your employees are doing. This doesn't mean you have to micro-manage. Just pay attention. Holding employees accountable isn't easy but it will make a significant impact on your leadership and business results. Use these tips to streamline the accountability process and make it an everyday part of your leadership.

Management Afterthought

If I could relive my early management years, I would do a lot of things differently. I would:

- Make more mistakes (I spent so many years trying to avoid mistakes when they are truly the building blocks for wisdom).
- I'd laugh more with my employees (it's a shame some of them will never know how truly funny I am).
- I'd be less gullible
- I would take a time management course way earlier

into my leadership role. (This was a life saver).
- I'd stop seeking permission and acknowledgement for validation.
- I would stop and breathe more.
- I would absolutely create healthier boundaries between my work and home life!

Nonetheless, I am grateful for all of my knowledge and my experiences. Is there anything that you would tell the younger you?

If so, write it on the next page. You may need your own words of wisdom a few years from now when you're running your own department.

Acknowledgements

I would like to first thank my shepherd and the overseer of life, without you none of this would be possible. To my husband Reginald Alderman, thank you for continuously supporting me in all that I do. You have stayed by my side through thick and through thin, and I am eternally grateful for your support.

To my children, Davon, Tamara, Tye, and Lyfe I thank you for helping me mature and develop into the woman I am today. You all give me the drive and the determination to make anything possible and all that I do is for you.

To my parents Mark and Karen Baker, I am forever grateful for the love and instruction that you have provided me, and now provide my children. Your love convinced me that this world was mine for the taking, and convinced me since childhood that "I'm The Boss" of my situation. It is because of your teaching that I was able to make it to this point today.

To my editorial team; Brandi, Jhaney, and Erica, I cannot express how grateful I am that you said yes to working on this project with me.

Last but not least, I want to say thank you to you! Thank you for embarking on this journey with me, and supporting my vision of empowerment. I hope that this book not only provided you with guidance, but also with the encouragement to know that you are the Boss of your kitchen.

I hope that Kie Ingredients to Success has left you feeling like a master chef in your enhancement kitchen.

Now let's get cooking!!!

Made in the USA
Columbia, SC
08 October 2020